Directions

You are about to learn how to play hockey.

Each chapter will have a test for you to show how much you've learned.

Begin by entering your name into your workbook.

_____

print your name

Chapter 1

DIVIDING THE ICE

the Forward's areas

Forwards

RIGHT WING   CENTER   LEFT WING

Forward's areas are the areas each Forward is responsible for.

Left Wing area	<ul><li>The line starts at the left post of your team's net</li><li>Goes to the face-off dot</li><li>Goes to the face-off dot at the other end of the ice</li><li>Goes to the post</li></ul> 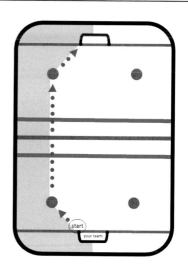
Center area	<ul><li>The lines start at both posts of your team's net</li><li>Goes to the face-off dots</li><li>Goes to the face-off dots at other end of the ice</li><li>Goes the posts</li></ul> 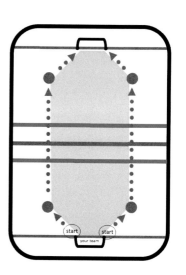
Right Wing area	<ul><li>The line starts at the right post of your team's net</li><li>Goes to the face-off dot</li><li>Goes to the face-off dot at the other end of the ice</li><li>Goes back into the post</li></ul> 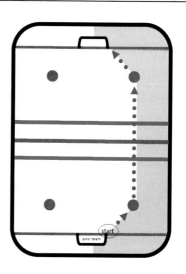

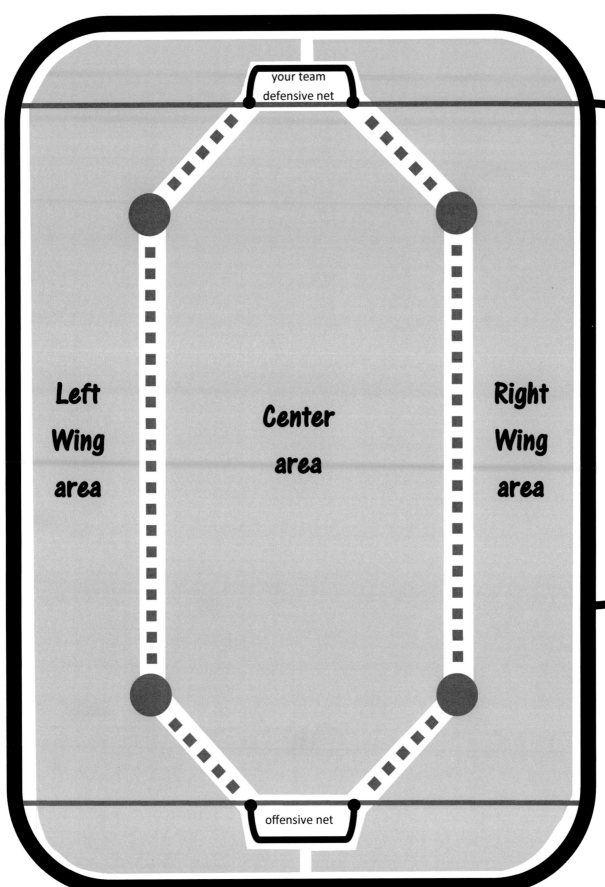

TEST #1

1. Draw the line for the Left Wing area.

2. Draw the line for the Right Wing area.

3. Draw the lines for the Center area.

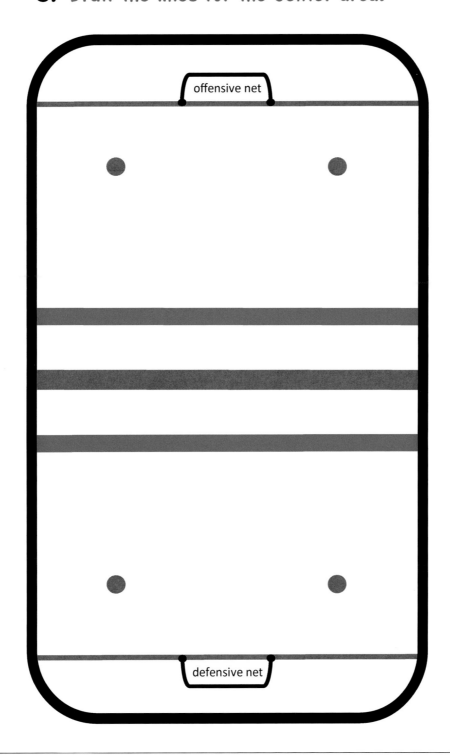

Chapter 2

DIVIDING THE ICE

the Defense areas

Defense

Right Defense

Left Defense

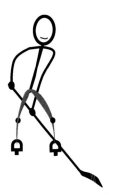

Defense areas

Left Defense line	<ul><li>Starts behind the defensive net</li><li>Down the middle of the ice</li><li>Ends one stick and arm's length past the blue line</li></ul> 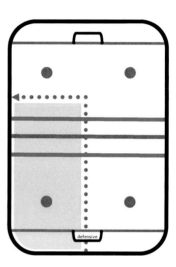
Right Defense line	<ul><li>Starts behind the defensive net</li><li>Down the middle of the ice</li><li>Ends one stick and arm's length past the blue line</li></ul> 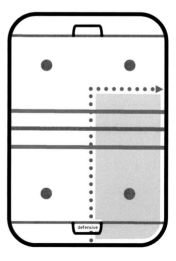

offensive net

Stick and arm's length

Stick and arm's length

Left

Defense

Right

Defense

Defense areas

defensive net

TEST #2

1. Draw the lines for the Left Defense area.

2. Draw the lines for the Right Defense area.

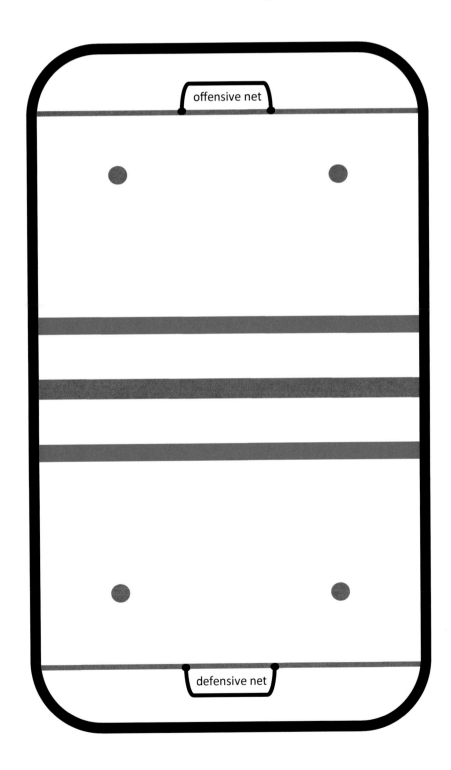

You have completed Chapter 1 and 2,
DIVIDING THE ICE.
FORWARDS AND DEFENSE

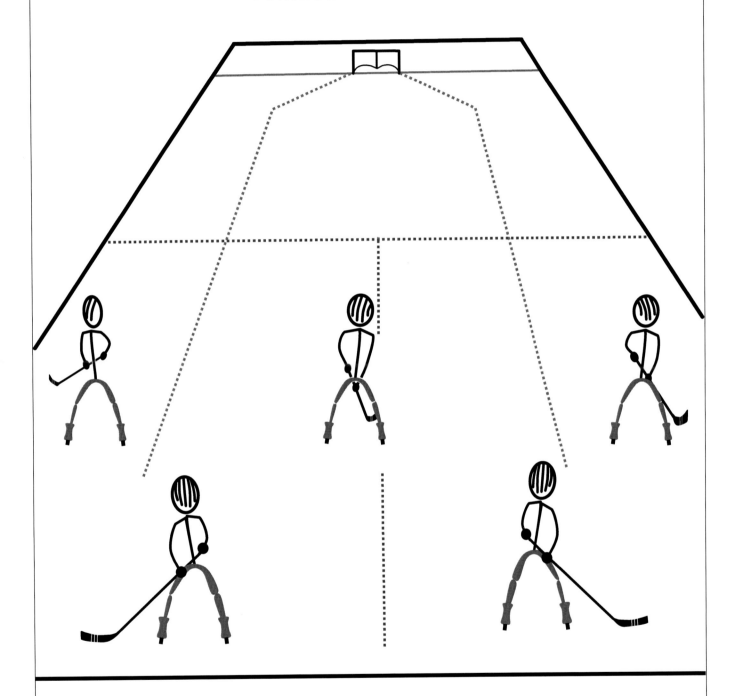

In the next chapter (the BREAKOUT) you will learn how to move the puck up ice.

Chapter 3

The BREAKOUT

The BREAKOUT is how to move the puck from your end to the other team's end.

1	A Defenseman sets up behind the net with the puck. The other Defenseman stands in front of the net.
2	The Wings slide into their Breakout spots (see opposite page). WHERE IS THE BREAKOUT SPOT? Across from the faceoff dots, back to the boards.
3	The Defenseman passes the puck to the Wing.
4	The Wing passes the puck along a 22.5 degree line to the Center.
5	The Center passes the puck to the other Wing.
6	This pattern continues until the Center has the puck in front of the net for a shot.
7	The Defensemen follow the Forwards up ice.

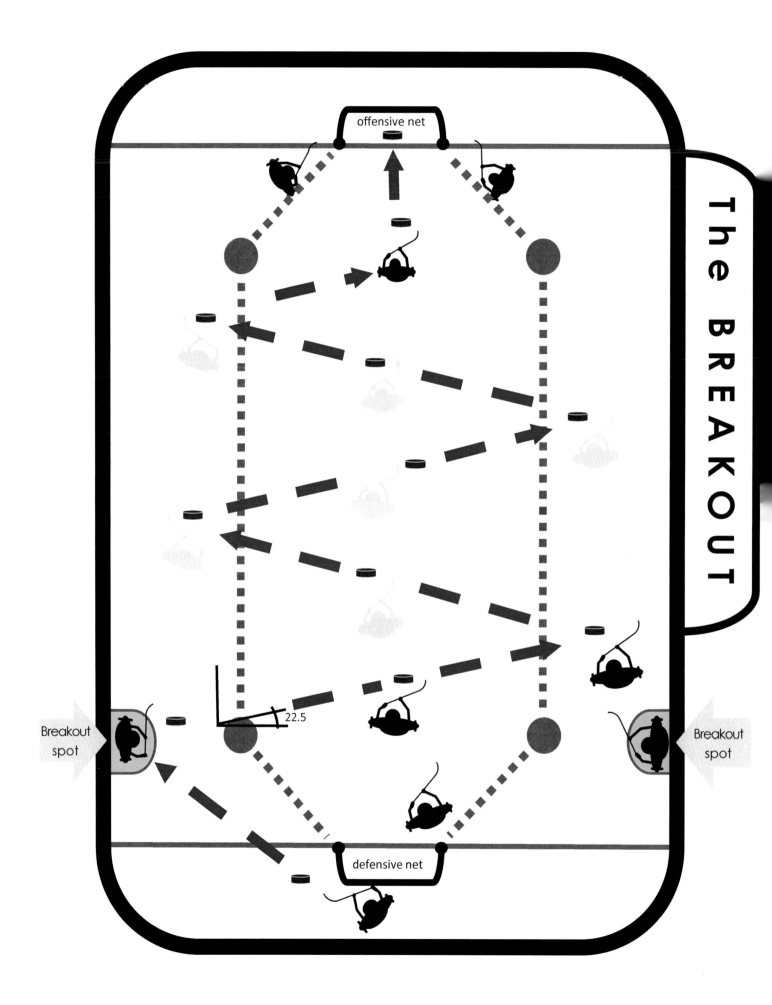

offensive net

The BREAKOUT

22.5

Breakout spot

Breakout spot

defensive net

TEST #3

1. Draw the BREAKOUT.

   Start with the puck behind the net.

   use: **L** for Left Wing - **C** for Center - **R** for Right Wing - **D** for Defense

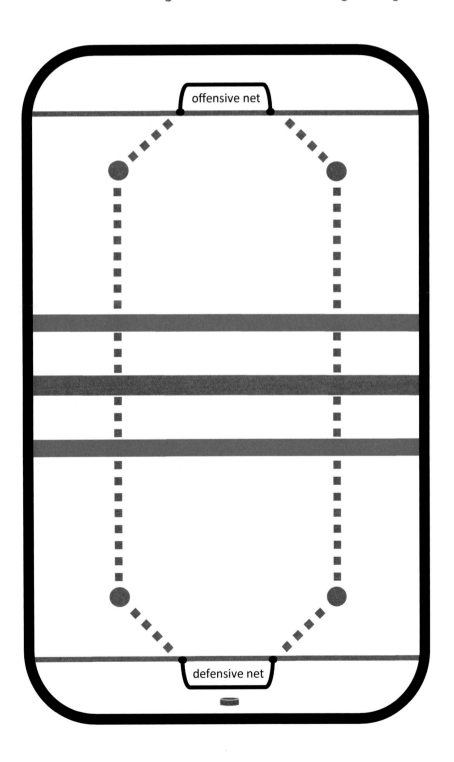

You have completed Chapter 3, the BREAKOUT.

In the next chapter (the RESET) you will learn what to do when the BREAKOUT has a problem.

Chapter 4

The RESET

The RESET is what your team does when the BREAKOUT breaks down.

1	When the BREAKOUT breaks down, the puck is re-gathered and passed back to the Defenseman.
2	The second Defenseman drops back to negative 22.5 degrees (see opposite page).
3	The Defenseman then passes the puck to the second Defenseman.
4	The second Defenseman passes up to the Wing.
5	The BREAKOUT continues on.
6	**NOTE:** All three Forwards may start a RESET. The Center may send the puck back to either Defenseman.

offensive net

breakdown!

-22.5

defensive net

The RESET

TEST #4

1. Draw the RESET.

   Show how your team handles a breakdown of the
   BREAKOUT. Begin with the breakdown at the blue line.

   use: **L** for Left wing - **C** for Center - **R** for Right wing - **D** for Defense

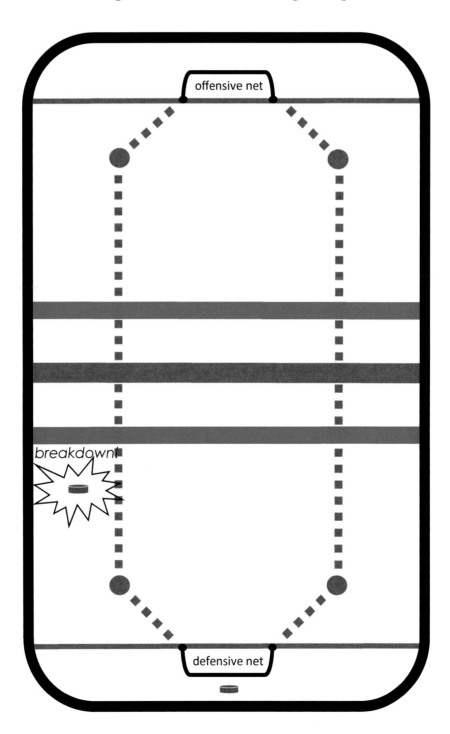

You have completed Chapter 4, the RESET.

negative 22.5

You have completed

the STRUCTURE of hockey

Forwards

Defense

Breakout

Reset

You now understand how hockey is played.

TOUCHES OF THE PUCK

Here are the numbers of passes you should expect to give and receive ?

per Breakout	2
per shift	4
per game	48
per season	1,440

Tips and Helpful Information

Tying Your Skates
Standing in Your Skates
Your Hockey Stick
Terms

TYING YOUR SKATES

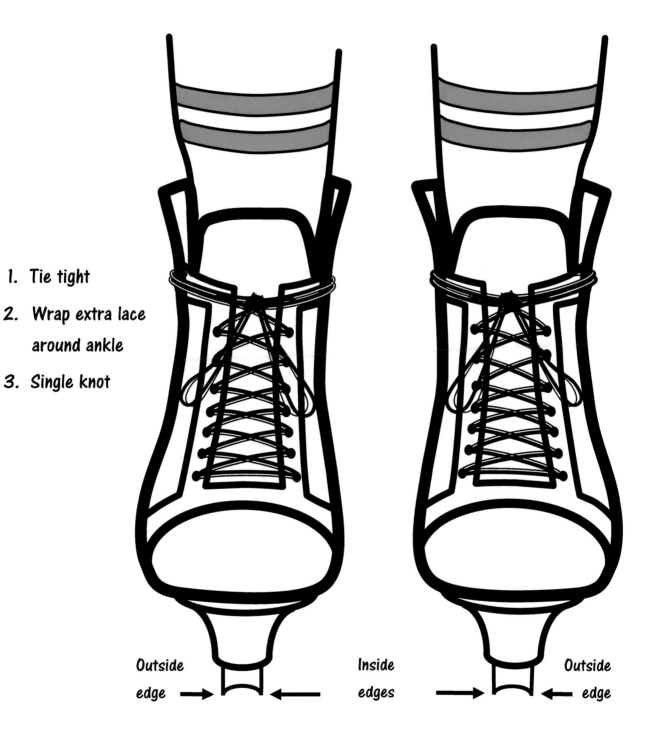

1. Tie tight
2. Wrap extra lace around ankle
3. Single knot

Outside edge →   ← Inside edges   Outside edge →   ← edge

STANDING IN YOUR SKATES

Correct

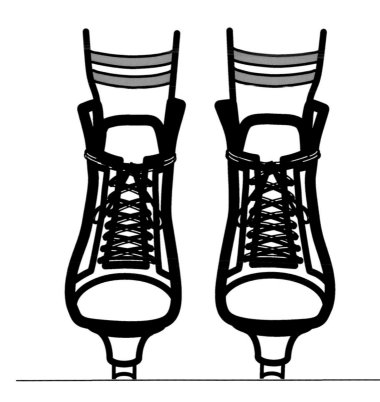

Incorrect

YOUR HOCKEY STICK

STICK HEIGHT

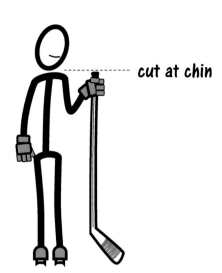

cut at chin

KNOB LENGTH

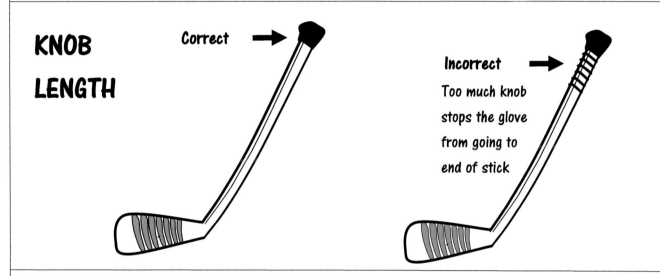

Correct →

Incorrect →

Too much knob stops the glove from going to end of stick

HOW TO HOLD

1. Hold stick straight up

2. Drop elbow on glove

3. Grab stick

4. That is where your hands should be

Terms

Breakout	Is how your team moves the puck from your end of the ice to the other team's end.
Breakout Spot	Is where the Wings set up for the Breakout. ACROSS FROM THE FACE-OFF DOTS, BACK TO THE BOARDS (SEE DIAGRAM 1)
Reset	Is what your team does when the BREAKOUT has a problem. You move the puck back to the Defenseman, over to the other Defenseman and up to the Wing.
22.5 Degree Line	The **line** the puck is passed along.

Diagram (1)

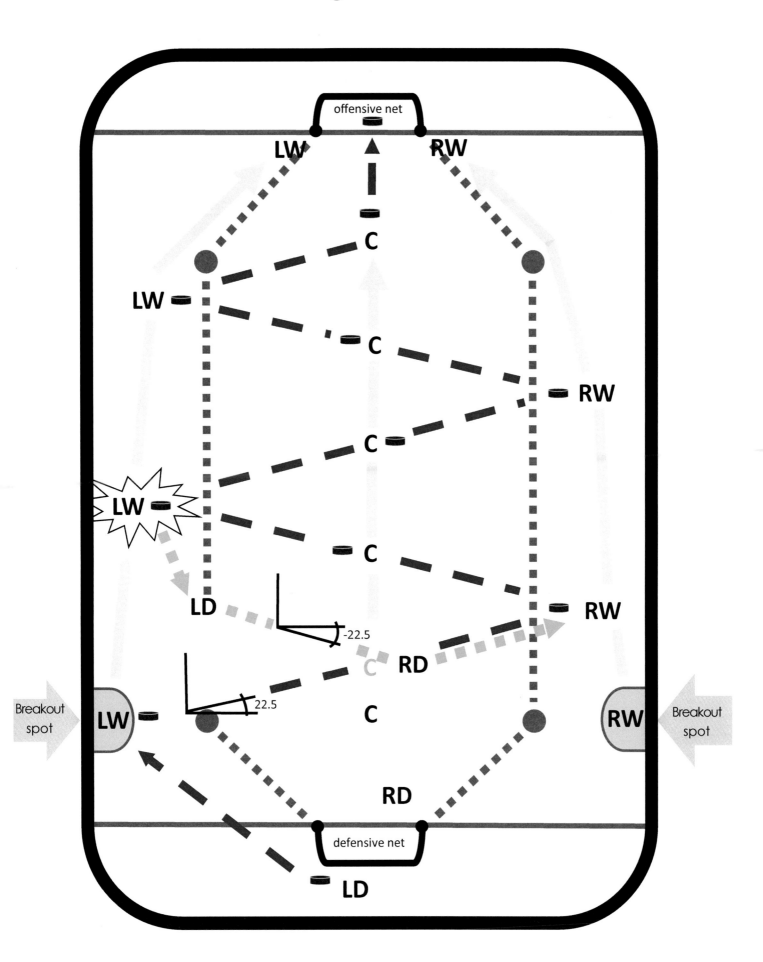

Terms

Defensive Zone	Your team's end, from the blueline to the boards. (see Diagram 2).
Neutral Zone	The area between the defensive zone and the offensive zone (blue line to blue line).
Offensive Zone	The opponent's end, from the blueline to the boards.
Shooting Area	Is where the Center sets up for a shot (see Diagram 2)
The Point	The area in the offensive zone where your team's Defensemen stand.

Diagram (2)

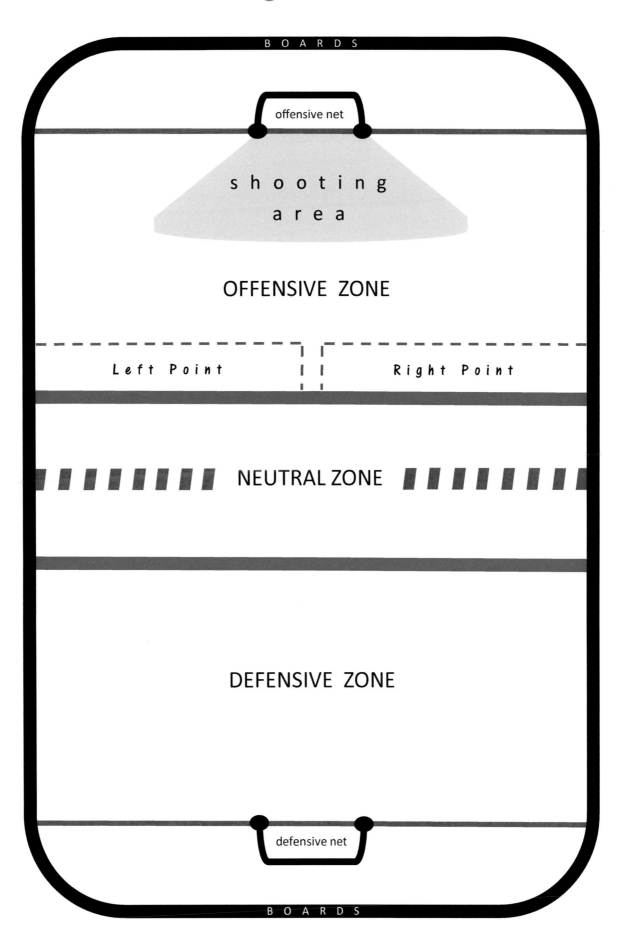

Made in the USA
Lexington, KY
26 May 2018